My Baptism Book

A Child's Guide to Baptism

Diana Murrie
Illustrations by Craig Cameron

CHURCH HOUSE
PUBLISHING

How to use this book

This book aims to help children understand baptism.

It may be read by an adult and child together, or be used in more formal baptism preparation with a family or an older child.

It also serves as a reminder of a child's baptism - one which a child may wish to return to again and again.

A book is an inanimate object. It can come alive only when it is opened at the first page.

Children, or those with limited reading skills, may need help to make this happen. This is best done by offering open questions, such as 'I wonder ...'; by talking about words and pictures, creating space for observation and reflection, where answers and opinions are all valued equally, and by the gentle encouragement to turn to the next page.

4

belonging

I wonder what 'belonging' might mean?

5

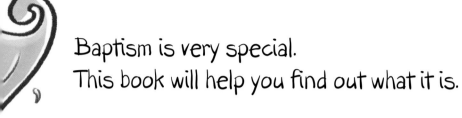

Baptism is very special.
This book will help you find out what it is.

What other things are really, really special to you?

People are baptized as

babies ...

children ...

young people or grown-ups.

How old are you?

7

People who love us take us to church to be baptized.

Church is a place where people who love God meet together.

8

People in church welcome us into God's family. This happens through baptism, as Jesus said.

When we are baptized, we are asked questions.

When we are baptized, we make promises.

These are very important.

What do you think a promise is?

Babies and little children who cannot answer for themselves have parents and godparents to answer the questions and make the promises for them.

Godparents promise

to love and pray for their godchild

to tell them about their baptism

to help them grow up to make the promises for themselves

They say they will

reject the devil
renounce evil
repent of sin

They say:

> 'I turn to Christ.
> I submit to Christ.
> I come to Christ.'

Everyone says:

> 'I believe in God the Father.
> I believe in Jesus Christ, his only Son.
> I believe in the Holy Spirit.'

When we are baptized, we are signed with the cross on our forehead.

Sometimes the sign of the cross is made with oil, but sometimes just with a finger or thumb.

The cross is invisible.

It cannot be seen, but it will always be there.

The sign of the cross helps us to remember that:

we belong to Jesus

he died for us

we promise to follow him

'Christ claims you for his own.'

'Receive the sign of his cross.'

Water is very special.
Without it we cannot live.
We use water in many ways ...

to drink ...

to wash ...

16

The water of baptism is ...

the water of creation ...

the water of freedom ...

This is the font.
It holds the water of baptism.

A special prayer is said over the water.
It begins

'We thank you, almighty God, for the gift of water to sustain, refresh and cleanse all life ...'

In baptism, water is poured on our head.

Sometimes, people are dipped in the water, or go down into it.

Names are very important in baptism.

What is your name?

We are baptized in the name of

'... the Father,
and of the Son,
and of the Holy Spirit.'

The Holy Spirit gives us new life and helps us follow Jesus.

The Holy Spirit

... moves like the wind

... flies and hovers like a dove

... burns with energy, like a living flame

... comes bringing comfort and power

... is invisible

23

Light helps us to see where we are going.

It helps plants and animals to grow strong and healthy.

Here are some lights.

Which ones can you see in the sky?

Which ones keep you safe?

Which ones help in the dark?

Which are party lights?

One day, some people asked Jesus,
'Who are you?'

He said 'I am the Light of the World.'

John 8.12

Jesus was baptized in the river Jordan.

Mark 1.9-11

25

When we are baptized, we become part of God's worldwide family - the Church.

Everyone says:

'We welcome you into the fellowship of faith;

We are children of the same heavenly Father;

We welcome you.'

Through baptism

we belong to God

we are members
of the family
of the Church

we are beginning
a new life

To help everyone remember

the promises ...

the sign of the cross ...

the water ...

the light ...

this baptism and their own

those who have been baptized may be given a candle.

'You have received the light of Christ;
walk in this light all the days of your life.'

And everyone says ...

'Shine as a light in the world
to the glory of God the Father.'

As you grow, you will find out more about this new beginning, getting to know God and learning how much he loves you and how much you can love him.

You can do this through:
- saying prayers and going to worship;
- finding out about the stories in the Bible;
- asking questions.

When you are older, you will make the baptism promises for yourself at confirmation.

Church House Publishing
Church House
Great Smith Street
London SW1P 3AZ

ISBN 978 0 7151 4303 2 (hardback)
ISBN 978 0 7151 4226 4 (paperback)

Published 2006 by Church House Publishing.

Eighth impression 2018

Cover design by Craig Cameron

Printed in England by Ashford Colour Press Ltd, Gosport, Hants